THE BATTLE OF
FIRST BULL RUN

The Civil War Begins

By **Larry Hama**   Illustrated by **Scott Moore**

rosen publishing's
rosen central®

New York

Published in 2007 by The Rosen Publishing Group, Inc.
29 East 21st Street, New York, NY 10010

First edition, 2007

Photo credits: p. 4 (top) Courtesy of Anne S. K. Brown Military Collection, Brown University Library; (bottom) Stratford Archives; p. 5 From an oil painting by John Robertson; p. 7 Courtesy of Anne S. Brown Military Collection, Brown University Library; p. 44 Public domain; p. 45 (top) Osprey Publishing; (bottom) Courtesy of Anne S. K. Brown Military Collection, Brown University Library

Geeta Sobha, Editor, Rosen Book Works
Simone Drinkwater, Series Editor/Osprey Publishing
Nel Yomtov, Series Editor/Rosen Book Works

Library of Congress Cataloging-in-Publication Data

Hama, Larry.
    The Battle of First Bull Run : the Civil War begins/by Larry Hama.— 1st ed.
    p. cm. — (Graphic battles of the Civil War)
    Includes bibliographical references and index.
    ISBN-13   978-1-4042-0776-9 (lib.)   978-1-4042-6476-2 (pbk.)
    ISBN-10   1-4042-0776-7 (lib.)   1-4042-6476-0   (pbk.)
    6-pack ISBN-13   978-1-4042-6271-3   6-pack ISBN-10   1-4042-6271-7
    1. Bull Run, 1st Battle of, Va., 1861—Juvenile literature. I. Title. II. Series.

E472.18.H23 2007
973.7'31—dc22

                                                              2006007283

CONTENTS

THE AMERICAN CIVIL WAR, 1861–1865

By the nineteenth century, many economic and political differences had developed between the Northern and Southern states in America. None was more important than the issue of slavery. In the South, slaves were needed to work in the plantations. Slavery was illegal in the North.

Tensions between the two sides grew. In 1860, Abraham Lincoln, an anti-slavery candidate, won the presidential election. The South felt threatened by Lincoln's victory. Soon, South Carolina seceded, or left, the Union. More Southern states followed. These states formed the Confederate States of America—a government separate from the United States of America. Americans on both sides feared that the tension would lead to war.

Finally, on April 12, 1861, Southern forces bombed Fort Sumter in South Carolina. America was at war. The historic first major battle of that struggle was fought at Bull Run, Virginia, on July 20, 1861.

KEY COMMANDERS

IRVIN McDOWELL
President Lincoln's third choice to command the Union army, he led at First Bull Run. Four days later, George McClellan replaced him.

PIERRE G. T. BEAUREGARD
Confederate brigadier general, he was in many key battles during the war. He commanded Confederate forces at the attack on Fort Sumter.

WINFIELD SCOTT
In 1861, Scott was commander of the Union. His plan to defeat the South eventually became the plan by which the North won the war.

THOMAS JACKSON
Commander who brought the South many victories before his death in battle. He earned the nickname "Stonewall" at First Bull Run.

O n April 12, 1861, Confederate artillery opened fire on Fort Sumter, a U.S. government fort in Charleston Harbor, South Carolina. After many years of bitter disagreement between Northern and Southern states, mostly over the issue of slavery, the divided nation was at war. President Abraham Lincoln's immediate problem was making Washington, D.C., the nation's capital, safe from Confederate attack. The city was nearly defenseless and was surrounded by slaveholding territory. Additionally, the capital of the newly formed Confederate States of America (CSA) was only 100 miles south of Washington, in Richmond, Virginia.

Lincoln called for 75,000 troops to serve for three months. Jefferson Davis, president of the CSA, asked for 100,000 troops to be raised by the Southern states that had seceded from the Union.

★ **Abraham Lincoln**

★ *U.S. President Abraham Lincoln faced t... challenge of keeping the Union together durin... the Civil War.*

Army camps soon sprang u... around both capitals. Troops on bo... sides were mostly untrained and wo... a confusing assortment of uniforms i...

lue, gray, brown, and green. Late in May 1861, Union troops occupied Alexandria, Virginia, across the Potomac River. Lincoln was hopeful about a Northern victory. He knew that he had to use force against the Confederates, but he believed that after one major battle the South would rejoin the Union.

Lincoln's 75-year-old commander, General Winfield Scott, believed differently. The 16,000 men of the prewar army were mostly in the West, fighting Native Americans. One-quarter of his officers had quit to join the Confederacy. State militias and volunteers would take at least six months to train. After that, Scott suggested they be used to secure the Mississippi River and then invade the South along the western rivers.

Meanwhile, the Union navy would blockade Southern ports. Finally, a year or two later, the Union forces would advance on Richmond. Northern newspapers ridiculed this as "The Anaconda Plan," because the strategy aimed to strangle the Confederacy slowly, like a snake smothers its prey. Lincoln only approved the blockade. He wanted to defeat the South in weeks, not years, and the three-month enlistments of his army were nearly up.

The Confederates were also optimistic. They thought that one big battle would surely mean one big Southern

★ **Jefferson Davis**

★ Jefferson Davis was elected president of the Confederate States of America (CSA) in February 1861.

victory, forcing the Union to accept the South's independence.

The Blue Ridge Mountain chain divided each army in two. In the Shenandoah valley, elderly Union general Robert Patterson faced Confederate general Joseph E. Johnston. East of the mountains, General Irvin McDowell commanded the main Union army. Confederate general P. G. T. Beauregard awaited him along the line of Bull Run Creek, in Virginia, covering the vital rail center at Manassas.

★ Five weeks after Lincoln became president, the Confederates opened fire on Fort Sumter, one of the last Union-held forts in the South.

On July 16, McDowell's army set out from its camps around Washington for Manassas, 25 miles away. His plan was to first gain control of the towns of Fairfax and Centreville, locate the Confederate army, and then attack it from a flank.

On July 18, McDowell sent General Daniel Tyler's division to sco[u] Blackburn's Ford, telling Tyler not [to] start a battle. However, Tyler ignore[d] the orders, and he attacked. Whe[n] Tyler found he was facing Beauregard[']s main force, he broke off the figh[t.] Now aware that an attack on th[e] Confederate right was impossibl[e,]

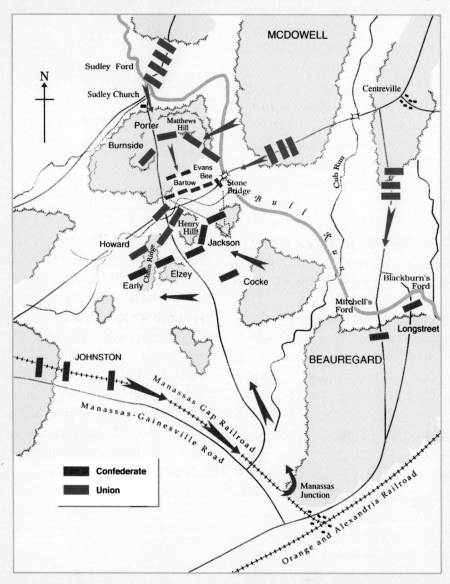

★ The Battle of First Bull Run, fought on July 21, 1861, was the first major land battle betwe[en] Union and Confederate armies. Union general Irvin McDowell crossed at Sudley Ford and attack[ed] the Confederates on Matthews Hill. Later in the day, Confederate reinforcements arrived to br[eak] the Union right flank. Defeated, the Union army fled the battlefield in chaos, eventually reachi[ng] the safety of Washington, D.C., on July 22.

McDowell began to prepare for one on the left.

Meanwhile, as McDowell occupied Fairfax on July 17, Beauregard telegraphed Johnston and asked him to move his force immediately to assist him. Unnoticed, Johnston concentrated his troops at Piedmont on the Manassas Gap Railroad and began shipping them 34 miles east. Each trip took five hours. His cavalry and artillery moved to Manassas by road.

At 2:00 A.M. on July 21, three divisions of McDowell's army left Centreville. Tyler's division advanced down the Warrenton Turnpike to Bull Run Creek. McDowell swung north to Sudley Ford with the other two divisions. Tyler got into position first, at 6:00 A.M., and opened fire across the bridge. McDowell would not be in position until 9:00 A.M.

Beauregard had expected another attempt on his right and concentrated his troops around Mitchell Ford. However, he got a surprise when a Confederate signal station observed McDowell's divisions advancing on his left. The only Confederate troops available to stop McDowell were those opposing Tyler at the Stone Bridge, commanded by Colonel Nathan Evans.

Evans marched to Matthews Hill and fought alone until Confederate General Barnard Bee joined him at 10:00 A.M. But by 11:30, Union troops had driven them from Matthews Hill. When Beauregard and Johnston arrived at noon, they saw they were in trouble. Johnston turned over command to Beauregard and concentrated on getting more troops.

The fight now centered on Henry Hill. McDowell's two divisions faced

★ **Gen. Irvin McDowell**

★ *Union general Irvin McDowell was an inexperienced commander at the battle of First Bull Run. His mistakes led to the Union's defeat.*

the broken remains of Bee's troops. But more Confederate units had arrived, including General Thomas Jackson's Virginia brigade.

Jackson held Henry Hill from 1:00 P.M. until 4:00 P.M. McDowell, trying to limit casualties, attacked one regiment at a time. Attempting to outflank Jackson, McDowell unwisely sent forward his artillery without infantry support. In another incident, a blue-coated regiment approached and the Union gunners let them come, only to discover they were Confederates when they were fired on. Captured Union guns changed hands five times over the next two hours.

At 4:00 P.M., two fresh Confederate brigades entered the fight. It was the end for the Union army. The exhausted Union troops had no fight left in them. They retreated in disorder to Centreville.

THE BATTLE OF FIRST BULL RUN

The Civil War Begins

ON APRIL 12, 1861, THE FIRST SHOT OF THE AMERICAN CIVIL WAR WAS FIRED AT THE UNION GARRISON IN FORT SUMTER, SOUTH CAROLINA.

THE MAN WHO FIRED THAT SHOT WAS 75-YEAR-OLD EDMUND RUFFIN, A FANATICAL SOUTHERN SUPPORTER.

NO ONE WAS KILLED DURING THE ATTACK. HOWEVER, A UNION SOLDIER DIED FROM AN ACCIDENTAL EXPLOSION IMMEDIATELY AFTER THE SURRENDER OF THE FORT.

THREE DAYS LATER, PRESIDENT ABRAHAM LINCOLN CALLED ON THE NORTHERN STATES TO RAISE 75,000 VOLUNTEERS FOR A THREE-MONTH ENLISTMENT.

ONLY THREE MONTHS?

IT WILL ALL BE OVER BY THE END OF SUMMER.

MEN RUSHED TO SIGN UP. SOME FELT PATRIOTIC OR HAD STRONG FEELINGS AGAINST SLAVERY.

JUST HAND ME A GUN AND POINT ME SOUTH!

...OTHERS THOUGHT IT WOULD BE A BIG ADVENTURE.

WEALTHY PEOPLE OFTEN FORMED VOLUNTEER REGIMENTS, WEARING CUSTOM-MADE UNIFORMS.

THE 11TH NEW YORK VOLUNTEER INFANTRY WERE CALLED FIRE ZOUAVES.

LINCOLN'S TOP COMMANDER, GENERAL WINFIELD SCOTT, HAD A PLAN.

WE SHALL TRAIN ALL SUMMER AND ATTACK DOWN THE MISSISSIPPI VALLEY IN THE FALL TO SPLIT THE CONFEDERACY IN TWO.

HOWEVER, NO ONE WANTED TO WAIT THAT LONG.

RAILROADS WERE THE SUPPLY LIFELINES OF BOTH ARMIES. WITHOUT THE RAILROADS THERE WAS NO WAY TO GET CROPS TO MARKETS OR SEAPORTS.

MANASSAS JUNCTION, VIRGINIA, WAS THE MEETING POINT OF TWO IMPORTANT RAIL LINES. ONE OF THEM WAS THE ONLY RAIL LINK BETWEEN RICHMOND AND THE SHENANDOAH VALLEY*

*THESE SUPPLY ROUTES WERE ESSENTIAL TO THE CONFEDERATE ARMY'S SURVIVAL.

GENERAL P. G. T. BEAUREGARD WAS IN CHARGE OF THE CONFEDERATE DEFENSES AT MANASSAS.

HE HAD 21,000 MEN AND LARGE NAVAL CANNONS IN POSITIONS THAT COVERED ALL THE APPROACHES TO THE MEETING POINT OF THE RAIL LINES.

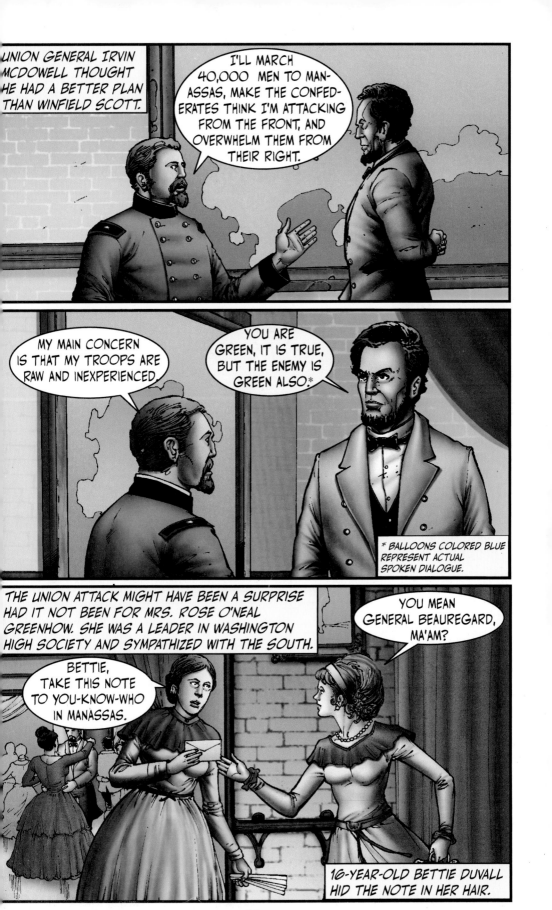

11

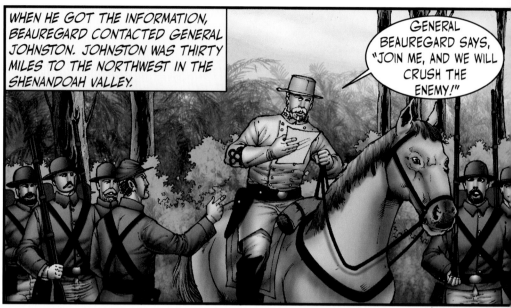

WHEN HE GOT THE INFORMATION, BEAUREGARD CONTACTED GENERAL JOHNSTON. JOHNSTON WAS THIRTY MILES TO THE NORTHWEST IN THE SHENANDOAH VALLEY.

GENERAL BEAUREGARD SAYS, "JOIN ME, AND WE WILL CRUSH THE ENEMY!"

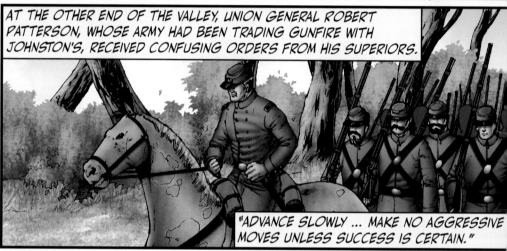

AT THE OTHER END OF THE VALLEY, UNION GENERAL ROBERT PATTERSON, WHOSE ARMY HAD BEEN TRADING GUNFIRE WITH JOHNSTON'S, RECEIVED CONFUSING ORDERS FROM HIS SUPERIORS.

"ADVANCE SLOWLY ... MAKE NO AGGRESSIVE MOVES UNLESS SUCCESS IS CERTAIN."

ON JULY 18, 1861, BRIGADIER GENERAL DANIEL TYLER LED THE FIRST UNION DIVISION TO REACH BLACKBURN'S FORD ON THE BULL RUN RIVER, JUST NORTH OF MANASSAS.

THIS IS GOING BETTER THAN EXPECTED.

HE HAD STRICT ORDERS FROM GENERAL MCDOWELL TO AVOID A FIGHT. TYLER WAS JUST TO KEEP UP THE APPEARANCE OF AN ATTACK FROM THE FRONT.

TYLER DISOBEYED ORDERS AND ATTACKED. HE MET SUCH LITTLE RESISTANCE THAT HE THOUGHT TOTAL VICTORY WAS WITHIN HIS GRASP.

HOWEVER, WHEN CONFEDERATE TROOPS BROUGHT UP MORE MEN, TYLER'S SOLDIERS BROKE AND RAN.

AN ARTILLERY FIGHT BROKE OUT. ONE CANNONBALL HIT THE MCLEAN HOUSE WHERE BEAUREGARD WAS HEADQUARTERED.

HOMEOWNER WILMER MCLEAN HAD HAD ENOUGH EXCITEMENT AFTER THIS. HE MOVED 200 MILES ACROSS THE STATE.

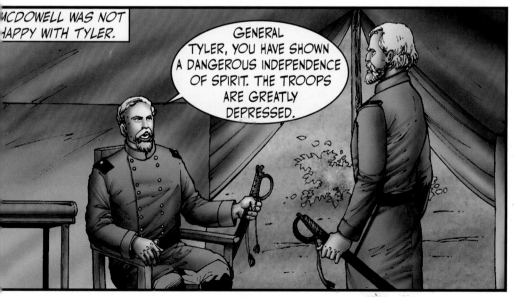

MCDOWELL WAS NOT HAPPY WITH TYLER.

GENERAL TYLER, YOU HAVE SHOWN A DANGEROUS INDEPENDENCE OF SPIRIT. THE TROOPS ARE GREATLY DEPRESSED.

MEANWHILE, PATTERSON WAS TRYING TO MOVE AN ENTIRE ARMY WHOSE THREE-MONTH ENLISTMENT WAS ABOUT TO END.

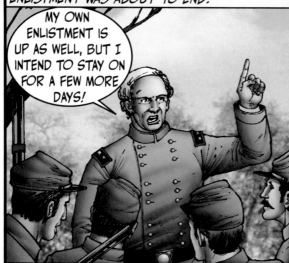

MY OWN ENLISTMENT IS UP AS WELL, BUT I INTEND TO STAY ON FOR A FEW MORE DAYS!

ON THE SAME DAY THAT TYLER ATTACKED AT BLACKBURN'S FORD, JOHNSTON STARTED TO MOVE HIS ARMY TO HELP BEAUREGARD AT MANASSAS.

THERE WAS ONLY ONE LOCOMOTIVE WITH SIX CARS.

GENERAL THOMAS JACKSON'S BRIGADE WAS THE FIRST TO ARRIVE.

WE MOVED THE WHOLE BRIGADE THIRTY-FOUR MILES IN JUST EIGHT HOURS, SIR! IT'S THE MODERN AGE, FOR SURE!

THE TRAIN WENT BACK FOR ANOTHER LOAD OF MEN.

ON JULY 20, PHOTOGRAPHER MATHEW BRADY ARRIVED AT MCDOWELL'S CAMP TO RECORD THE BATTLE FOR HISTORY.

IN WASHINGTON, SOME PEOPLE RENTED CARRIAGES TO GO SEE THE EXPECTED UNION VICTORY. THEY THOUGHT IT WOULD BE A COLORFUL SHOW.

MCDOWELL'S SCOUTS REPORTED TO HIM...

SIR, THE ROADS TO THE CONFEDERATE RIGHT ARE NOT PASSABLE.

THEN MY ORIGINAL PLAN WON'T WORK.

MCDOWELL'S NEW PLAN WAS TO FAKE AN ATTACK AT THE CONFEDERATE CENTER. THEN HE WOULD BRING HIS MAIN ASSAULT AROUND FROM THEIR LEFT.

THEN TWO DIVISIONS UNDER GENERALS HUNTER AND HEINTZELMAN ARE TO START MARCHING THE LONG WAY AROUND AT 2:00 A.M. ...

NONE OF THIS STOPPED MCDOWELL FROM ENJOYING AN ENORMOUS DINNER.

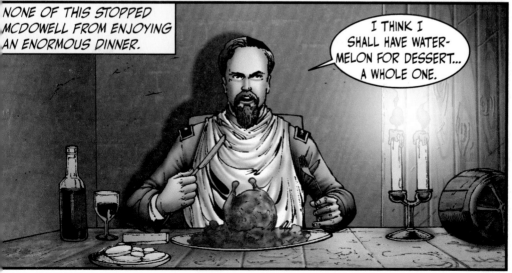

I THINK I SHALL HAVE WATER-MELON FOR DESSERT... A WHOLE ONE.

AT 6:00 A.M. ON JULY 21, TYLER LED THE INITIAL ATTACK AT THE STONE BRIDGE ON THE BULL RUN RIVER.

REMEMBERING MCDOWELL'S SCOLDING, TYLER DID NOT PRESS THE ATTACK AS HARD AS HE SHOULD HAVE.

I THINK NOT.

SIR, WE OUTNUMBER THE ENEMY SEVEN TO ONE! WE CAN TAKE THE OPPOSITE BANK, AND...

THE COMMANDER OF THE CONFEDERATES AT THE STONE BRIDGE WAS COLONEL NATHAN G. EVANS.

EVANS GREW SUSPICIOUS...

COLONEL EVANS, WHY DON'T THEY JUST TAKE THE BRIDGE?

THEY ARE NOT TIMID. IT MUST BE A PLAN.

16

HUNTER AND HEINTZELMAN WERE STUCK ON A NARROW PATH THAT WENT THROUGH THICK WOODS. IT HAD TO BE CLEARED AND WIDENED BY HAND.

WE ARE ALREADY THREE HOURS BEHIND SCHEDULE!

THEIR GUIDE MADE A WRONG TURN, WHICH ADDED THREE MILES TO THEIR ROUTE.

MCDOWELL WAS FEELING SO ILL, HE HAD TO RIDE IN A CARRIAGE AT FIRST.

OWW, IT MUST HAVE BEEN THE MELON.

BEAUREGARD'S CHIEF SIGNAL OFFICER, CAPTAIN E.P. ALEXANDER, HAD PUT UP LOOKOUT TOWERS AT IMPORTANT POINTS.

A LITTLE BEFORE 9:00 A.M., ALEXANDER SAW SUNLIGHT SHINING ON CANNONS AND BAYONETS FAR TO THE NORTH.

IT'S A UNION COLUMN! AT THE FORD BY SUDLEY SPRINGS!

COLONEL EVANS! A MESSAGE FROM CAPTAIN ALEXANDER— "LOOK OUT FOR YOUR LEFT. YOU ARE TURNED."

I KNEW IT!

EVANS LEFT FOUR COMPANIES TO COVER THE BRIDGE. THEN HE RUSHED TO HIS LEFT AS FAST AS HE COULD.

HURRY, MEN!

HE TOOK UP A GOOD POSITION ON MATTHEWS HILL AND WAITED

AT 9:15 A.M., THE 1ST RHODE ISLAND REGIMENT UNDER UNION COLONEL AMBROSE BURNSIDE MARCHED OUT OF THE WOODS INTO EVANS'S RANGE OF FIRE.

AAARGH!

GENERAL HUNTER WAS WOUNDED. HE GAVE COMMAND TO BURNSIDE.

I LEAVE THE MATTER IN YOUR HANDS.

IT WAS HUNTER'S 59TH BIRTHDAY.

BURNSIDE'S HORSE WAS SHOT OUT FROM UNDER HIM.

ALTHOUGH BURNSIDE THOUGHT HE WAS FACING A LARGE FORCE, HE DIDN'T BACK DOWN.

EVANS KNEW HE COULD NOT HOLD HIS POSITION MUCH LONGER.

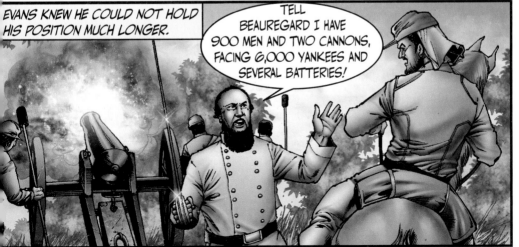

TELL BEAUREGARD I HAVE 900 MEN AND TWO CANNONS, FACING 6,000 YANKEES AND SEVERAL BATTERIES!

HELP FOR EVANS ARRIVED IN THE FORM OF GENERAL BARNARD BEE AND COLONEL FRANCIS BARTOW. THEY LED REGIMENTS FROM ALABAMA, MISSISSIPPI, AND GEORGIA.

BEE AND BARTOW FORMED UP IN A BATTLE LINE TO EVANS'S RIGHT.

WE MUST SILENCE THE NORTHERN CANNONS OR WE ARE FINISHED.

EVANS, BEE, AND BARTOW LED A DARING CHARGE AGAINST THE NORTHERN ARTILLERY.

SUPERIOR NUMBERS AND FIREPOWER FORCED THE CONFEDERATES BACK TO THEIR ORIGINAL POSITIONS.

ONE SOUTHERN SOLDIER DESCRIBED THE SCENE AS "A WHIRLWIND OF BULLETS."

20

UNION GENERAL S.P. HEINTZELMAN ARRIVED AT MATTHEWS MILL WITH HIS DIVISION AT ABOUT 11:00 A.M. MCDOWELL, WHO WAS FEELING MUCH BETTER, GAVE HIM ORDERS.

USE YOUR FRESH REGIMENTS TO KEEP UP PRESSURE ON THE ENEMY.

I'LL ORDER A FRONTAL ATTACK, SIR.

THAT ATTACK WAS BEATEN BACK.

A SECOND ATTACK WAS MOUNTED BY THE 11TH NEW YORK VOLUNTEER FIRE ZOUAVES AGAINST EVANS'S FLANK.

THAT ATTACK WAS BEATEN BACK AS WELL.

THERE'S A BIG DUST CLOUD TO THE NORTH, COLONEL EVANS!

ANOTHER UNION BRIGADE! WE'LL HAVE TO FALL BACK.

THE DUST WAS BEING CHURNED UP BY THE 3,400 FRESH TROOPS UNDER UNION GENERAL WILLIAM TECUMSEH SHERMAN.

AMONG SHERMAN'S BRIGADE WERE REGIMENTS WEARING GRAY VOLUNTEER MILITIA UNIFORMS.

LET'S SHOW THEM WHAT WE'RE MADE OF IN WISCONSIN!

THE 4TH ALABAMA UNDER GENERAL BEE WAS CONFUSED. THEY HELD THEIR FIRE.

DON'T SHOOT! THOSE ARE OUR BOYS OUT THERE!

AAAARGH!

THEIR CONFUSION PROVED TO BE FATAL

EVANS LED THE CONFEDERATE RETREAT.

FORM UP BY THAT HOUSE ON THE NEXT HILL TO THE SOUTH!

THAT WAS THE HENRY HOUSE.

THE FIGHT FOR HENRY HOUSE HILL WAS TO BE THE MAIN EVENT OF THE FIRST BATTLE OF BULL RUN.

WE'RE NOT BEATEN YET, BOYS.

MCDOWELL WAS CERTAIN THAT THE OUTCOME WAS ALREADY DECIDED.

VICTORY! THE DAY IS OURS!

HE SPOKE TOO SOON.

EARLIER THAT MORNING, A 650-MAN PRIVATE CONFEDERATE ARMY RAISED BY WEALTHY SOUTH CAROLINIAN WADE HAMPTON HAD ARRIVED AT MANASSAS JUNCTION.

THEY MARCHED AND RAN THREE HOURS IN THE BLAZING JULY HEAT TO GET TO HENRY HOUSE HILL.

ALTHOUGH STRONGLY OUTNUMBERED, THE HAMPTON LEGION HELD OFF THE UNION ADVANCE

THE LEGION WERE SOON FORCED TO RETREAT BACK UP THE HILL.

BUT THEY HAD BOUGHT PRECIOUS TIME. MORE HELP WAS ARRIVING FOR THE CONFEDERATES

24

INSIDE THE HENRY HOUSE, 84-YEAR-OLD JUDITH HENRY LAY ON HER SICKBED ATTENDED BY HER WHEELCHAIR-BOUND SON.

WHAT'S ALL THAT NOISE OUT THERE?

WHILE THE HAMPTON LEGION WAS MAKING ITS STAND, GENERAL THOMAS JACKSON ARRIVED WITH 2,000 VIRGINIANS AND FOUR CANNONS.

THEY ORGANIZED INTO A LINE 150 YARDS BEHIND THE FORWARD CREST OF THE HILL.

GENERAL BEE REPORTED TO GENERAL JACKSON...

THE ENEMY IS BEATING ME BACK, GENERAL JACKSON.

VERY WELL, GENERAL BEE.

HOW DO YOU EXPECT TO STOP THEM?

WE'LL SHOW THEM THE BAYONET. I'M TIRED OF THIS LONG-RANGE WORK!

BEE RALLIED THE ALABAMA REGIMENT WITH THE NOW FAMOUS QUOTE:

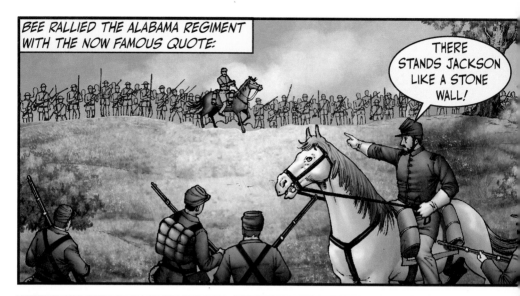

THERE STANDS JACKSON LIKE A STONE WALL!

FROM THEN ON, THE GENERAL WAS KNOWN AS STONEWALL JACKSON.

GENERAL BEE LED THE ALABAMA REGIMENT BACK INTO THE LINE OF FIRE. HE WAS KILLED BY A UNION CANNON BLAST.

THERE ARE SOME WHO SAY THAT WHAT GENERAL BEE REALLY MEANT WAS NOT SO FLATTERING TO JACKSON.

THERE HE STANDS LIKE A STONE WALL. WHY ISN'T HE HELPING US?

AROUND 12:30 P.M., BOTH BEAUREGARD AND JOHNSTON ARRIVED AT HENRY HOUSE HILL.

THEIR ACCOUNTS OF THE SAME EVENTS CONFLICT IN EVERY WAY.

BEAUREGARD'S REPORT IS COLORFUL AND ARROGANT. IT MAKES HIM SEEM HEROIC AND CLEVER.

PLANT THE FLAGS OUT FRONT! IT ENCOURAGES THE TROOPS!

JOHNSTON'S VERSION IS MORE MODEST AND PROBABLY MUCH TRUER TO THE ACTUAL EVENT.

THE CIRCUMSTANCE HAS BEEN GREATLY EXAGGERATED.*

*MEANING THAT THE CONFEDERATES WERE NOT IN GREAT DANGER.

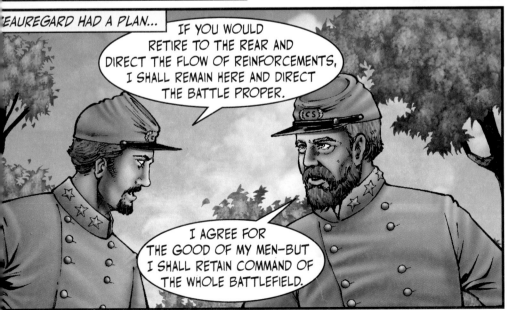

BEAUREGARD HAD A PLAN...

IF YOU WOULD RETIRE TO THE REAR AND DIRECT THE FLOW OF REINFORCEMENTS, I SHALL REMAIN HERE AND DIRECT THE BATTLE PROPER.

I AGREE FOR THE GOOD OF MY MEN—BUT I SHALL RETAIN COMMAND OF THE WHOLE BATTLEFIELD.

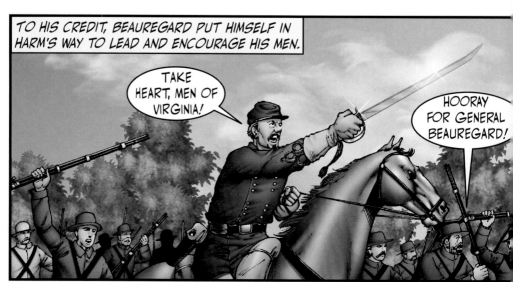

TO HIS CREDIT, BEAUREGARD PUT HIMSELF IN HARM'S WAY TO LEAD AND ENCOURAGE HIS MEN.

TAKE HEART, MEN OF VIRGINIA!

HOORAY FOR GENERAL BEAUREGARD!

BEAUREGARD'S HORSE WAS KILLED BY A BURSTING SHELL. THE SHOT ALSO BLEW THE HEEL OFF THE GENERAL'S BOOT.

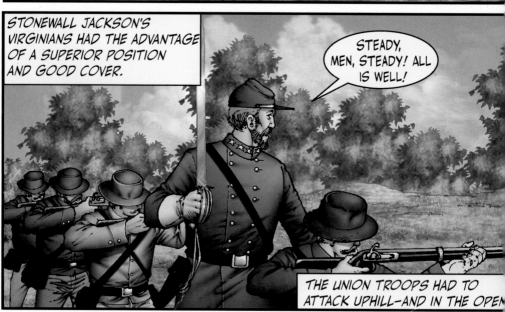

STONEWALL JACKSON'S VIRGINIANS HAD THE ADVANTAGE OF A SUPERIOR POSITION AND GOOD COVER.

STEADY, MEN, STEADY! ALL IS WELL!

THE UNION TROOPS HAD TO ATTACK UPHILL—AND IN THE OPEN

MCDOWELL LOST THE ADVANTAGE FOR THE UNION BECAUSE HE DID NOT ORDER A CHARGE ATTACK WHEN MOST OF HIS TROOPS HAD ARRIVED AT HENRY HOUSE HILL.

INSTEAD, HE HAD THE REGIMENTS CHARGE ONE BY ONE—FIRST THROUGH CANNON FIRE ...

... AND THEN INTO A DEADLY HAIL OF CONFEDERATE MUSKET FIRE AT CLOSE RANGE.

AS THE UNION TROOPS WERE DRIVEN BACK, ANOTHER REGIMENT WOULD BE SENT UP THE HILL TO GET THE SAME TREATMENT.

THIS GAVE THE CONFEDERATES PLENTY OF TIME TO RELOAD.

MCDOWELL MADE ANOTHER SERIOUS MISTAKE. HE ORDERED TWO OF HIS BEST ARTILLERY BATTERIES TO SET UP CLOSE TO THE HENRY HOUSE ...

... AND FORGOT TO SUPPLY INFANTRY TO PROTECT THEM.

THE BATTERIES, COMMANDED BY CAPTAINS CHARLES GRIFFIN AND JAMES RICKETTS, WENT UP UNSUPPORTED.

I HAVE BEEN TOLD THAT THE 11TH NEW YORK IS ON THE WAY.

I AM DUBIOUS.

WHILE GRIFFIN AND RICKETTS SET UP, BEAUREGARD MOVED HIS CONFEDERATES CLOSER TO THE CREST OF THE HILL ...

... MAKING IT MORE DIFFICULT FOR THE UNION CANNONS TO HIT THEM.

CONFEDERATE SHARPSHOOTERS IN THE HENRY HOUSE SHOT AT RICKETTS'S BATTERY AS THEY SET UP.

RICKETTS TURNED HIS CANNONS ON THE HOUSE AND FIRED.

THAT SHOULD KEEP THEIR HEADS DOWN.

ONE SHOT SMASHED JUDITH HENRY'S BED AND KILLED HER.

AS PROMISED, THE 11TH NEW YORK VOLUNTEER FIRE ZOUAVES MARCHED UP HENRY HOUSE HILL TO SUPPORT GRIFFIN AND RICKETTS.

THE CONFEDERATES HELD THEIR FIRE UNTIL THE ZOUAVES WERE TOO CLOSE TO MISS.

... AND THEN LET LOOSE A POWERFUL VOLLEY.

MOST OF THE BULLETS WENT OVER THEIR HEADS.

THE INEXPERIENCED SOUTHERN TROOPS HAD AIMED TOO HIGH.

KEEP YOUR HEADS DOWN, LADS! STEADY!

TWO COMPANIES ON THE RIGHT OF THE ZOUAVE LINE BROKE AND RAN.

THE FLEEING ZOUAVES WERE MET BY J.E.B. STUART'S CONFEDERATE CAVALRY, WHO HAD RIDDEN AROUND FROM THE SIDE OF THE HILL.

CAPTAIN IMBODEN, COMMANDER OF JACKSON'S ARTILLERY BATTERY, HAD BAD NEWS FOR THE GENERAL.

SIR, I REGRET THAT WE ARE OUT OF AMMUNITION—

GENERAL, YOU ARE WOUNDED!

A MERE SCRATCH.

THE UNION REGIMENTS KEPT ATTACKING IN WAVE AFTER WAVE.

DESPITE HIS WOUND, JACKSON WAS BEGINNING TO RELISH THE FIGHT.

GENERAL, THE DAY IS GOING AGAINST US!

IF YOU THINK SO, SIR, YOU HAD BETTER NOT SAY ANYTHING ABOUT IT.

CONFEDERATE COLONEL ARTHUR CUMMINGS LED THE 33RD VIRGINIA AGAINST THE UNION ARTILLERY.

THEIR BLUE UNIFORMS CONFUSED SOME UNION SOLDIERS

GRIFFIN WAS STOPPED FROM FIRING ON THEM BY HIS SUPERIOR OFFICER.

DON'T SHOOT! THOSE ARE OUR BOYS, COMING TO SUPPORT US!

NO, THOSE MEN ARE CONFEDERATES!

GRIFFIN LATER SAID, "THAT WAS THE LAST OF US. WE WERE ALL CUT DOWN."

RICKETTS WAS BADLY WOUNDED. HE WAS LATER ATTENDED TO BY BEAUREGARD'S PERSONAL SURGEON.

THE CONFEDERATES CAPTURED ALL TEN CANNONS AND ALL THE AMMUNITION.

TWO REGIMENTS OF MASSACHUSETTS VOLUNTEERS TOOK BACK THE BATTERY FOR THE UNION SIDE.

JACKSON AND HIS VIRGINIANS CHARGED, AND POSSESSION OF THE GUNS RETURNED TO THE CONFEDERATES. BEAUREGARD WENT ALONG WITH THEM.

GIVE THEM THE BAYONET!

THE 1ST MICHIGAN CAME UP THE HILL AND RECLAIMED THE BATTERY FOR THE UNION.

BY THE END OF THE DAY, THE SAME CANNONS HAD CHANGED HANDS FIVE TIMES.

BECAUSE OF DELAYS, INCLUDING THE SHOOTING OF AN ENGINEER, THE LAST CONFEDERATE REGIMENTS FINALLY ARRIVED BY TRAIN AT MANASSAS IN THE AFTERNOON OF JULY 21.

CONFEDERATE GENERAL KIRBY SMITH MARCHED HIS BRIGADE AT DOUBLE-TIME TOWARD THE SOUND OF THE GUNS.

HIS BRIGADE CONSISTED OF THE 1ST MARYLAND, THE 3RD TENNESSEE, AND THE 10TH VIRGINIA.

MINUTES AFTER ARRIVING AT HENRY HOUSE HILL, SMITH WAS SHOT THROUGH THE CHEST.

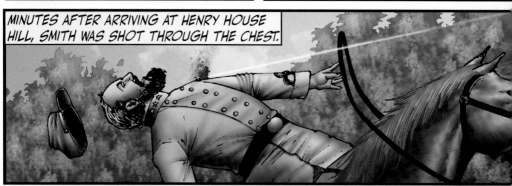

COLONEL ARNOLD ELZEY TOOK COMMAND. HE MARCHED HIS THREE REGIMENTS STRAIGHT TO THE FRONT.

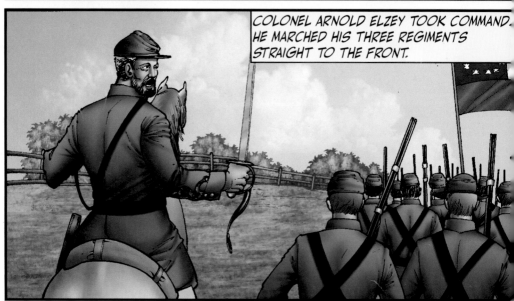

ELZEY'S BRIGADE CAME UPON A UNION LINE OF BATTLE ON THE CREST OF A HILL. THEY GAVE THEM A TREMENDOUS COMBINED VOLLEY.

FIRE!

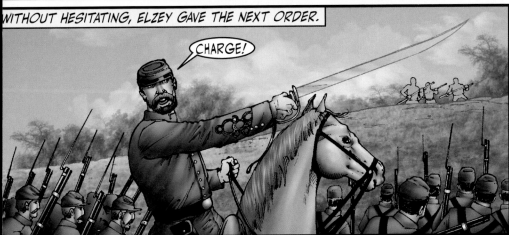

WITHOUT HESITATING, ELZEY GAVE THE NEXT ORDER.

CHARGE!

THE UNION TROOPS HAD BEEN ON THEIR FEET FOR 14 HOURS. THEY HAD BEEN UNDER FIRE FOR 6 OF THOSE HOURS.

THEY BROKE AND RAN.

THIS WAS THE TURNING POINT OF THE BATTLE—AND BEAUREGARD KNEW IT.

HAIL ELZEY!

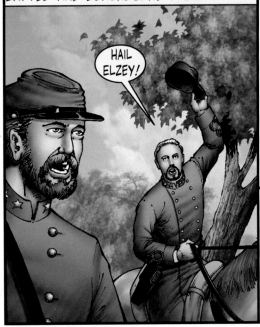

THE ENTIRE RIGHT SIDE OF THE UNION LINE COLLAPSED.

WE'RE WHIPPED! THE CONFEDERATE CAVALRY IS COMING!

THE CAVALRY?

THE PANIC SPREAD UNTIL MOST OF THE UNION ARMY WAS TRYING TO FLEE BACK TO WASHINGTON.

RUN! THE CAVALRY IS COMING!

ONLY ONE BATTALION OF REGULAR INFANTRY STOOD ITS GROUND. IT COVERED THE SHAMEFUL RETREAT OF THE OTHERS.

SHERMAN WAS DISGUSTED AT THE BEHAVIOR OF HIS MEN ...

... ALTHOUGH BEAUREGARD LATER WROTE THAT SHERMAN'S TROOPS MADE "A STEADY AND HANDSOME WITHDRAWAL."

A CROWD OF CIVILIANS, INCLUDING SENATORS AND THEIR FAMILIES, HAD COME FROM WASHINGTON TO WATCH THE BATTLE.

THEY WERE PICNICKING ON BOTH SIDES OF THE WARRENTON TURNPIKE, ABOUT A MILE WEST OF CENTREVILLE.

EVERYONE WAS PANICKING.

THE WARRENTON TURNPIKE WAS THE MAIN ROAD USED BY THE FLEEING UNION SOLDIERS.

CONFEDERATE ARTILLERY ADDED TO THE FEAR AND CONFUSION.

WAGONS AND CARRIAGES WERE ABANDONED. PEOPLE RAN SCREAMING ACROSS THE COUNTRYSIDE.

IN CENTREVILLE, MCDOWELL SENT A TELEGRAPH MESSAGE TO WASHINGTON.

THE DAY IS LOST. SAVE WASHINGTON AND THE REMNANTS OF THIS ARMY. THE TROOPS WILL NOT REFORM.

IN WASHINGTON, PRESIDENT LINCOLN RETURNED FROM HIS EVENING CARRIAGE RIDE AND WAS TOLD THE BAD NEWS.

LINCOLN LISTENED IN SILENCE, WITHOUT THE SLIGHTEST CHANGE OF FEATURE OR EXPRESSION ...

... AND WALKED QUIETLY AWAY TO ARMY HEADQUARTERS.

NION COLONEL DIXON MILES, OMMANDING THE 5TH DIVISION, WAS SUPPOSED TO FORM A LINE TO DEFEND CENTREVILLE...

.. BUT HE WAS TOO DRUNK TO ISSUE THE ORDERS.

JEFFERSON DAVIS, PRESIDENT OF THE CONFEDERACY, TOOK TWO TRAINS FROM RICHMOND TO MANASSAS JUNCTION AND RUSHED TO FIND JOHNSTON AND BEAUREGARD.

ON THE WAY, HE RAN INTO COLONEL ELZEY AND PROMOTED HIM TO GENERAL ON THE SPOT.

SOMETIME AFTER 10:00 P.M., DAVIS ASKED IF THE ENEMY WERE BEING PURSUED.

HE WAS TOLD THAT NO ONE HAD GIVEN THE COMMAND.

41

UNION GENERAL PATTERSON NEVER GOT HIS ARMY TO THE BATTLE. A LOT OF BLAME WAS PLACED ON HIM.

MCDOWELL WAS DEMOTED AND REPLACED BY GENERAL GEORGE B. McCLELLAN.

GENERAL SHERMAN THOUGHT HIS CAREER WAS OVER BUT IT WAS NOT.

BEAUREGARD WAS PROMOTED AND SONGS WERE WRITTEN ABOUT HIM. HE ENJOYED HIS NEWFOUND GLORY.

GENERAL JOHNSTON SAID, "THE CREDIT IS DUE TO GOD AND OUR BRAVE SOUTHERN SOLDIERS, NOT TO ME."

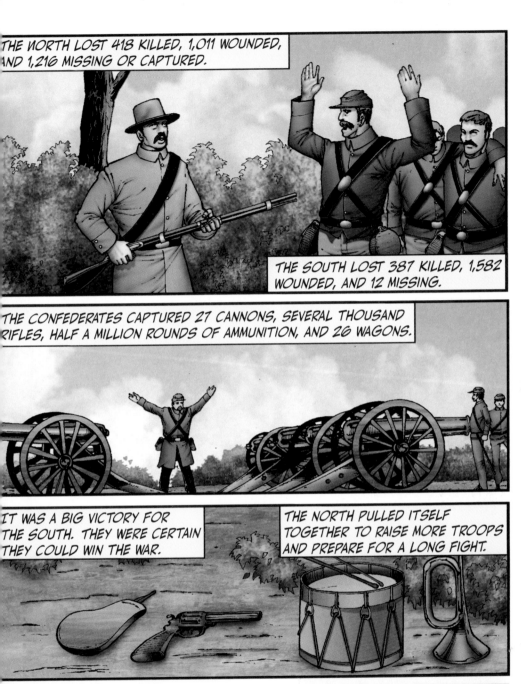

THE NORTH LOST 418 KILLED, 1,011 WOUNDED, AND 1,216 MISSING OR CAPTURED.

THE SOUTH LOST 387 KILLED, 1,582 WOUNDED, AND 12 MISSING.

THE CONFEDERATES CAPTURED 27 CANNONS, SEVERAL THOUSAND RIFLES, HALF A MILLION ROUNDS OF AMMUNITION, AND 26 WAGONS.

IT WAS A BIG VICTORY FOR THE SOUTH. THEY WERE CERTAIN THEY COULD WIN THE WAR.

THE NORTH PULLED ITSELF TOGETHER TO RAISE MORE TROOPS AND PREPARE FOR A LONG FIGHT.

AFTER THE BATTLE, WILMER MCLEAN MOVED TO APPOMATTOX COURT HOUSE, VIRGINIA.

ON APRIL 19, 1865, AFTER FOUR MORE YEARS OF WAR AND 600,000 DEAD, ROBERT E. LEE SIGNED THE CONFEDERATE SURRENDER IN MCLEAN'S LIVING ROOM.

THE END

Immediately following the Union loss, the mood in Washington was grim. However, it gradually changed. Shock was replaced by anger, and anger with determination. The day after the battle, as soldiers still staggered into Washington in a pouring rain, Lincoln called for 500,000 three-year volunteers. By the end of the week, the U.S. Congress had doubled that number.

Much of the blame for the defeat fell on Lincoln himself. The same newspapers that had demanded "On to Richmond" now blamed Lincoln for pressuring McDowell to advance. Though a commission had cleared McDowell, the army still blamed him for the defeat. He was replaced by the ambitious General George McClellan.

In the South, the battle seemed to confirm the belief that it took only a few Southerners to whip any number of "Yankee" clerks and storekeepers. In fact, the two sides had been evenly matched: 35,000 Union troops faced 29,000 Confederates, with only about 18,000 on each side actually fighting. General Stonewall Jackson would later comment that it was too bad the South had won the first battle so easily. The North drew strength and unity from defeat; the South learned nothing from victory.

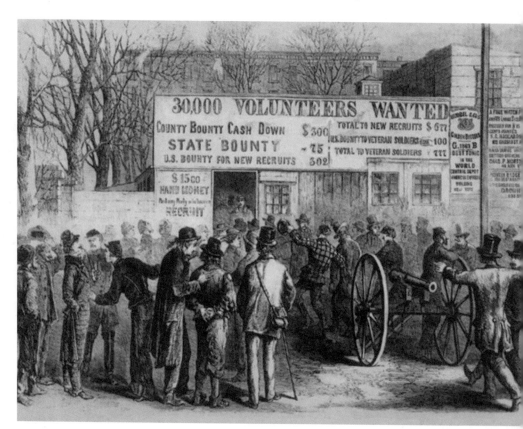

★ *After First Bull Run, the Union realized that the war would go on far longer than they had first thought. The government quickly called for volunteers to join the army.*

The Confederates thought that their flag looked too much like the Union flag. Confederate General P. G. T. Beauregard designed this new battle flag.

Though the South was the victor at Manassas, their men were no more experienced than the Northern soldiers. Despite the lack of training on both sides, however, the majority of troops did not run. They took casualties and fought on. One of every nine Confederates in battle was killed or wounded, compared to one in every six Union soldiers. As the armies learned their grim trade in the months and years ahead, casualties mounted into the tens of thousands. Seen in the larger context of the Civil War, the battle of Manassas, or First Bull Run, with its shocking 5,000 casualties, was a minor skirmish.

The battle had other effects. The Union army immediately got rid of their gray and nonstandard uniforms. In the South, noting that the Confederate national flag was vaguely similar to the Northern flag, General Beauregard designed a new battle flag, which was adopted by the army.

Disputes also arose over the naming of the battle. Normally the victor names the battle. The Confederates called it Manassas after the nearest town. The North refused to accept this and named it after the nearest body of water, Bull Run Creek. This practice would continue through the rest of the war, giving most battles two names.

★ The Union retreated from the battle, in shock at the harshness of the fight. Both sides suffered many casualties.

artillery Large, heavy guns that are mounted on wheels or tracks.

battalion A large body of soldiers organized as a unit; two or more battalion form a regiment.

battery A grouping of artillery pieces.

blockade The closing off of an area to prevent movement of people and supplies.

brigade A large army unit.

column A formation in which soldiers are placed one behind the other.

commission A group of people who meet to solve a problem or do certain tasks.

company A group of soldiers led by a captain.

crest The top part of a mountain or hill.

dubious Feeling or showing doubt.

enlistment An agreement to join the armed forces.

exaggerate To describe something as being larger than it is.

fanatical Being unreasonably enthusiastic.

flank The far left or right side of a body of soldiers.

flatter To praise in a way that is not sincere.

garrison The troops stationed at a military base.

hail To pour down like a shower.

legion A large group or number of people or things.

pursue To chase in order to catch.

regiment A unit of troops made up of two or more batallions.

remnant A small group of survivors.

secede To formally withdraw from a group or organization, often to form another organization.

skirmish A minor fight between small bodies of troops.

volley A discharge of bullets from a gun.

volunteer A person who does a job freely and usually without pay.

Zouave A soldier who dressed like a French infantryman; the uniforms were very brightly colored.

★ For More Information ★

ORGANIZATIONS

Manassas Museum
101 Prince William Street
Manassas, VA 20110
(703) 368-1873
Web site: www.manassascity.org/index.asp?NID=41

Manassas National Battlefield Park
2521 Lee Highway
Manassas, VA 20109-2005
(703) 754-1861
Web site: www.nps.gov/mana/

FOR FURTHER READING

Carter, Alden R. *The Civil War: American Tragedy.* New York: Scholastic Library Publishing, 1992.

Davis, William C. *First Blood: Fort Sumter to Bull Run.* Alexandria, VA: TIME-LIFE BOOKS, 1983.

Hankinson, Alan. *First Bull Run 1861: The South's First Victory.* Oxford, England: Osprey Publishing, 1990.

Kops, Deborah. *Battle of Bull Run.* San Diego, CA: Blackbirch Press, 2001.

⋆ Index ⋆

WEB SITES

Due to the changing nature of Internet links, the Rosen Publishing Group, In has developed an online list of Web sites related to the subject of this boo This site is updated regularly. Please use this link to access the list:

http://www.rosenlinks.com/gbcw/fbr